Wisteria from Seed

Wisteria from Seed

Jeremy Cantor

Kelsay Books

ISBN-13: 978-0692320808

Cover photograph: Arcandina (PhotoFlickr)

Kelsay Books
Alabaster Leaves Publishing
www.kelsaybooks.com

To

my sons, Noah and Toby

my granddaughter, Abigail Tabitha

the world's best daughter-in-law, Kat

and my wife, Marsha,

without whom

life would be a language without metaphor

Contents

III

The End of the Tourist Season

Foreword

Jeremy Cantor's collection, *Wisteria from Seed,* frustrates categorization in most dimensions that commentators find comfortable. It's principally free verse, but not assiduously unmetered; it doesn't eschew rhyme; it's both objective (to the point of clinical) and deeply personal; it has a strong through-current of scientific naturalism (with a pronounced predilection for ornithology); and it often reads as fluidly as prose. Rhetorically, it finds universals in the quotidian, insinuating the reader into Cantor's personal narrative, its meaning disguised in the plain dress of moment-to-moment experience. In these ways, the work is truly modern, or perhaps contemporary is the better word, in the sense that all of the post-Post-Modern arts have relaxed their self-restraints and admitted a stylistic and technical eclecticism that was strictly impermissible only a few decades ago. In the same way that representation has reentered the visual arts or that tonality and older notions of formalism have been reintroduced to music, classical attributes of poetry have found their way into current expression alongside the cherished attribute of freedom, which is its modern legacy.

From the present volume, take "Sculpture," which is free yet all but strictly iambic; "Well-Mannered Thief" is canonical iambic pentameter blank verse whereas "Mother Instinct" mixes feet of different types in meters of varying lengths; "Differential Diagnosis" is (self-mockingly) rhyming free verse but "Fallow" reads like prose. That prosaic style is highly developed in poems like "The Full Set" and "Display Case," which read to me like Faulkner, but not stream-of-consciousness so much as stream of reflection. Imagery can be concise to the edge of crispness, as in "Deference" and "The End of the Tourist Season," or vivid, voluble, almost reckless, as in "Changing Seasons."

The poet as observer is fundamental to the modern art, so where distinctions among poets must be partly measured in such qualitative and technical terms, they're only useful insofar as they assay the voice, the character, the affect and effect of the artist as well as the richness of their subjects—all of these melding in the act of reading. For the casual reader, modern poetry must accomplish two things at the outset: it must be parseable, and it must leave an immediate, even if superfluous, impression. For the reflective or recidivist reader, it steeps in the sub-conscious, bleeding upward as its submerged meaning finds resonance, then inference in the individual mind. In good poetry, reading is as urgent to the activation of the poem as was its writing. This collection is, in that sense, very, very good.

—Michael Manning
former Classical Music Critic/Arts Correspondent
The Boston Globe
October, 2014

I

A Little Night Music

last night until dawn
kept awake by mockingbird
reviewing old poems

Partnership

Now that I've invited you into my studio
where my most delicate work is on display
where even a brush with the tip of your scarf
might bring something, shattered,
to the floor at your feet
I must remind myself I asked for help with this.
I know that I would never finish it
without you.

So here you are at work.

It's nearly done. Almost everything I want to say,
it says.

Please forgive me if sometimes I get nervous
and yes, I'll admit it, even a bit jealous
watching you smoothing an edge here,
changing a word there.

Wisteria from Seed

"Almost no one grows wisteria from seed,"
I told my sons.
"This one has a healthy set of leaves
so it ought to flower
in about ten years."

I'm sixty now.

When I was in school
a botany professor showed our class
a bamboo plant.
"This flowers every forty years," he said.
"I won't be here to finish the experiments
I might start now.
If any of you are planning graduate studies,
please see me after class.
I've got some ideas I'd like to try."

I never thought myself a man of faith
yet I grow wisteria from seed
while others study bamboo
plant vineyards
grow olives
raise children.

Tamarind

I woke beneath the tree the Arabs call
the Date of India, beneath the tree
the Indians call the Imli.
I should not sleep here
where the dry pods of the tamarind
click against each other in the wind.

This is the tree whose fallen fruit
so bruised the walking feet of Radha
that she cursed it for delaying her
as she went to be united
with her love, Lord Krishna,
cursed it so its fruits would never ripen—
to this day the fruit falls to the ground
only half-ripe, still soft.

On the mountain slopes that face the sea
in Oman, the tamarind grows wild.
The Portuguese and Spaniards
took it everywhere they went.
The ghosts of India went everywhere
the tamarind was taken
and it gathered local ghosts
wherever ghosts were found.

The locals tell you not to walk beneath
the tamarind—the ghosts appear at night
but still I chose that place to sleep.

I listened as ghosts wailed
and whispered stories,
their stories and mine, I listened to them all.

Now that night has passed, come sit by me
beneath the tamarind, and I will do my best
to tell to you a few ghosts' tales—
their stories and mine, I like to tell them all.

The Full Set

Why thank you
yes, they are beautiful aren't they
my grandmother brought them over from Warsaw
they were made in Czechoslovakia, see here underneath
she left because she had to of course
things had just gotten too ugly
she was so happy when she met my grandfather
and so was he, they thought that
now they would be happy, now they would
always have what they
always had been missing
of course they stayed together later
in spite of it all
that's what people did

No, those are fruit bowls
the others got broken
I only have three and I haven't been able
to find replacements, not even at those places
where the serious collectors go
they have the big plates and the saucers and
the occasional gravy boat and creamer but
never the pieces I'm looking for
odd, isn't it
no I don't think it's just me not at all
it seems like everybody breaks
the same pieces.

Display Case

Regretting that I could not stay to watch
as you put final touches to your canvas
I saw you through the window of your shop,
your shop pushed to the edge by the Depression.
(Fresh-cut blooms no longer paid the rent.)
You'd filled your shop with your own canvasses
all along the walls up to the ceiling.

Earlier, in daylight, I'd stopped by
to say hello—you'd left your door unlocked.
Too intent on painting to remember
to put your keys back in your pocket, you'd
just left them on the counter. I'd gone
in back and found you at your painting.
I'd kept my visit short, just long enough
to risk paint on my jacket with a hug
which you'd also kept short, holding in place
a solid brick of air between our bodies,
an empty space that might have meant to say,
Not now, I'm painting, please don't interrupt,
or *Not now, no, not ever, we're both married,*
or maybe just *That's all I have to give.*

Now, in your window as the darkness fell
you sat painting in your empty shop
your back turned toward the street,
working with your palette knife and brush.
A bit of thinner on the corner of
a rag caressed the canvas while I watched.
I did not stay. (I was expected elsewhere.)

Were you at your place in the front room
because it had become too cold out back?
Or had you picked that spot to advertise
your painting and yourself to passersby?
Or were you waiting for a special friend—
working where you'd easily be found
your door intentionally left unlocked
(but not, of course, for me)?

Why Don't You Finish Anything You Start?

The untrained dog flushes a bird
but she does not know there is
something she is supposed to wait for,
a way these things are done,
so she chases it, barking at the sky
until she flushes another
which she chases until
she flushes another
and so across the field,
right, left, back, away,
back and away again
chasing another and another
until she lies down exhausted
not far from where she started,
having brought back
nothing.

She will be here again tomorrow.
Together we will run
and run.

What This Dog Thinks

I do not know whether dogs can think, or what thinking is, or whether human beings can think. But whether human beings can think or not, I know that those who love dogs think that dogs can think. This, I am afraid, is the sum total of my contribution to human knowledge on this important subject.
— Bertrand Russell, "Do Dogs Think?" (1932)

I don't know what dogs think.

Today I watched a woman throw a ball
for a pair of Boston terriers to retrieve.

There was a moment
when I thought I saw
a shadow of a thought
cross a canine face.

"If I drop the ball in front of my dogfriend
instead of in front of my human packleader
will my dogfriend pick it up and throw it for me?"

But it passed.

I don't know what dogs think.

Books have been written
on the subject of what dogs think
but I have not read them.

There are guesses I could make
about what a dog has never thought,
such as "Why *is* the velocity of light in a vacuum constant
regardless of the relative velocities of the source and the
observer?"

But that's an easy game.

No,
what I really wonder is
how often dogs think
about how life might be different

as one dog may have thought
just before she slipped her collar and ran off
never to be seen by me again.

Tough Times

I wasn't the first guy
to get out of school in the middle of a recession
that had people standing in line
or sitting in hiring halls or just giving up
and sitting on the stoop all day

to find out there wasn't any work
requiring a mind or even decent
eye-hand coordination or just a loud voice

but for a while I wondered—

was I the first guy who got a gig washing dishes
who skipped his lunch break to look good
to the supervisor even though the slop
was raining onto his shoes because the
garbage disposal in the IHOP's kitchen
was not just broken but busted wide open
while the lowlife manager and his pal
lifted $2K from the drop safe with a
coat hanger and then blamed it on
the guy at the sink with the slop
raining onto his shoes and the cops
bought the story for a while
but finally decided it was a setup—

no

happens to everybody these days.

Chilly Night

I woke up cold
having thrown off the covers in my sleep
and got ready to go to work.

Last night
those with no bed or roof or job
slept on benches, under shrubs, in parks,
over steam grates.

One winter morning
when I was a child
my aunt turned the ignition key
and we heard a short ghastly animal scream.
She climbed out, looked under the hood,
and said, "Stay in the car.
You shouldn't see this."

This afternoon
in the washroom
two other men
slipped into easy conversation about sports,
the male lingua franca I will never learn.

I would rather talk about how
this morning on my way to work
as I drove around a corner
and into the glare of the sun
I suddenly saw on my windshield
cat paw prints.

Fisherman's Line

I

The hummingbird feeder
I bought her on Valentine's Day
is getting lots of use.

I wonder aloud if they know I bring their food.
She says *Of course, silly!*
You know what Willie would have said!

From the kitchen table she watches their
courtship, quarrels and acrobatics
while she drinks her morning coffee.

As I sit across the table from her,
my back to the window,
she gazes past me
at the hummingbirds,
fascinated by what I can't see.

II

Fishing had kept Willie from the streets
when he was young—
his brothers and his childhood friends
all dead or in jail.

When I told him the bluegills
in Whiskeytown Lake
saw through my every move
and bit everything but the hook,
he laughed, *Everything's got a brain!*

Yesterday I watched my inline spinner
sail out and away,
farther than I'd ever cast before.
My knot had come untied,
and the lure was following
its long and perfect arc,
at last unencumbered.

Introduction to Crop Management

Ag School, Bachelor's Degree Program

Time! Pencils down.

I have not had time to write down
everything I know about tomatoes

indeterminate tomato plants
live until first frost
losing their summertime enthusiasm
through shortening days

indeterminate tomato plants
lean against their stakes,
bowing beneath the weight
of fruit that won't have time to ripen.

Aerial Survey

The hawkmoth knows
she will have to provide for her offspring
somewhere else

she sees that my tomato plants
are guarded by a forest of alyssum
whose flowers are already drawing
the tiny parasitic wasps
whose children would devour hers
were she so foolish
as to lay
her eggs nearby
she doesn't even have to think it over

but it rained very hard last night
and I still believe
that as she flies past my garden
she takes a bit of comfort
at the sight of the rain-crushed alyssum
beaten flat against the earth
looking like that forest in Siberia
after the Tunguska Event.

Mother Instinct

We needed a jackhammer to plant roses.
The hard adobe earth refused the shovel,
so to plant our shrubs we hired a man
to bring an auger on a half-ton truck.
We built stone walls with what his drilling had
brought up, like parodies of old New England
farmers clearing land for pasture.

Our house was in a windy corridor
on an unprotected hilltop.
I grew accustomed to the wind;
my wife did not.
Late one night a roaring gale
dragged her from sleep.
Through our younger child's window
she watched the merciless wind
whip our youngest tree about.

She threw a jacket over her nightgown
and went outside to save *Acer palmatum*,
driven by pity for a battered living thing.
She picked up the rocks I'd stacked around the birches,
carried them across the yard
and built a new wall
that would shield the little tree from wind.
The work was hard, the night was dark,
the wind blew leaves and dirt,
snapped twigs around her face and snarled her hair,
but couldn't interrupt the midnight rescue.

I slept through all of it.

Fallow

There will be no crop this year
the unused earth will do whatever it wants
it will grow what the wind blows, the birds drop
and the shaggy creatures shake from their coats
it will pool in the rain and bake in the sun
the birds, the insects and the wind
will complete the flowers' lovemaking
and the grasses
if left friendless by the mower
will spread themselves, out of our sight,
to rise elsewhere in tall green crowds
where none are lonely.

Vocal Mimicry

The Northern Mockingbird's mimicry is likely to serve as a form of sexual selection....As convincing as these imitations may be to humans, they often fail to fool other birds, such as the Florida Scrub-Jay.
—N. T. Owen-Ashley, S. J. Schoech, R. L. Mumme,
    Context-specific response of Florida Scrub-Jay pairs to
    Northern Mockingbird vocal mimicry, *The Condor* 104 (2002)

THE MOCKINGBIRD

the male mockingbird
isn't fooling anyone —
still, females love it

THE MOCKINGBIRD'S NEIGHBOR

What do the other birds think they should think
when they hear the male mockingbird sing?
Ornithologists say that it's not for the robin,
the chickadee, towhee, woodpecker or scrub-jay
but for competitors in his own species
and for his long-sought-after mate.

But what does the scrub-jay in the next tree think,
hearing a song that's so nearly his own?

"Oh, that song he is singing...
it sounds *so* familiar!
reminds me of something I can't quite remember —
a feeling, perhaps,
that I felt
when I stood in this treetop last year
and called to my love
and built last year's nest
and raised last year's brood
and sang last year's
last song?"

31

Revisiting

This seaside town
where we used to bring the children
is one huge garden

as after a long drink of water
on a hot day
my eyes are full

tonight
when I close my eyes
I will see flowers
leaves
surf

I ask her, "How do you feel?"

"Something is breaking," she says,
"like ice in the spring."

Sculpture

I dreamed that I was made of sand
and you tried to shape me with your hands

upon your first attempt I slid apart
and fell into the angle of repose

your second try was better, and I kept
a roughly human form for several minutes
before I slipped again into a heap

with each additional attempt your hands
learned something new and worked with love and patience
but not until your touch had reached perfection
did all the unconnected parts turn one
and all the disconnected grains turn flesh
and all the waste and windblown become me.

The Nietzsche Contrapositive

You went off your pain meds
having decided that you would rather
have mental clarity than anything else

that is consistent with
all I know about you
I would find it admirable

were I not married to you
were I not daily wishing for nothing
but to feel all of your skin
touching all of mine at once

(Then Aristotle looked up from reading *Götzen-Dämmerung*
and said, *According to this book,*
that which does not make me stronger kills me.)

II

First Date with Athena

the owl at sunset
let me see her great wings spread
too early, she thought

Differential Diagnosis

Doesn't anyone know
what was wrong with Van Gogh?

Bipolar disorder, absinthe, epilepsy
lead paint toxicity or apoplexy
acute intermittent porphyria
syphilis or gonorrhea
digitalis OD, or just the DT's
Ménière's disease or schizophrenia?

As for myself
I have no excuse.
(I don't even have you.)

Harp String

By road we reached a convenient parking spot
where a yard-wide strip of earth divided the pond in two

I was a junior and she was a senior

We held opposite ends of a stalk of grass in our teeth
and listened to the different notes it made as we plucked it,
varying the tension by how hard we pulled away from each other

I never told her
that for that one day
I loved her.

Lengthwise

Pinot needs constant care and attention. You know? And in fact it can only grow in these really specific, little, tucked away corners of the world.
　　—Paul Giamatti as Miles Raymond in *Sideways* (2004)
　　　Alexander Payne, director

We did the Valley lengthwise, north to south.
Calistoga down to Napa, easy
if you take it easy on the wine.

"Did you see the one
who poured the first flight of dry reds?
Those eyes could melt a man at twenty paces!
But I couldn't ask her out.
She's at work—
awkward for her, you know?"

"You could have given her your card," I told him.

"Why bother?
I'm not even in her league."

Another mile in silence
then a winery with roses at the end
of every row of comfortably old vines,
grapes hanging, waiting for the picking
and the crush.

The gates had closed at five
so it was easy to admire the wrought-iron tracery
against the background of the cellars, vines
and roses.

"Nice gates," he said.

I pointed out, "They're closed."

"That's how I know they're nice," he said,
cradling the bottle he'd just bought,
wishing he had sprung for the reserve.

Lessons from the Spring

grebe (order Podicipediformes): *In nearly all courtship ceremonies, the roles of the sexes are interchangeable. The same is true of the precopulatory displays, and reverse mounting has been reported for all species that have been thoroughly studied.*
—Robert W. Storer, *The Encylopædia Britannica* (online)

A Brewer's blackbird
whistled a wedding march
for the pair of mourning doves
mating in the still-bare Chinese tallow tree
while below, a white-crowned sparrow
industriously kept the floor clean

Watching the ceremony taught me
which one of the pair was the male,
but only for a moment

Had they instead been western grebes
caressing each other with
green leaves held in dagger-like bills
exchanging a reassuring glance with blazing scarlet eyes,
rushing headlong across the water side-by-side
then eagerly taking turns
I would not have known
even that.

Deference

Not just later,
when the universe turns insideout
overandoverandover

but from the moment
when mind
with an understanding nod
kindly steps to the wings
and leaves the stage to breath and skin

everything else disappears.

Nightsong and Sunrise

The mockingbird sings every song he heard when he was young.
When he's not singing he is dancing:
fly straight up, then float back down,
flash the white wing bars and flick the tail!

He has a few songs of his own, songs he was born with.
Perhaps he's written a few new ones, too. (My ear is not
so finely-tuned an instrument that I can tell.)

We talked of songs of mockingbirds that night,
of clever stratagems of crows and ravens,
and of the dreams of captive parrots.

That night you told me there's no death,
only a change. I would have liked—
no, would have loved—to be convinced,
but I wasn't, and I doubt I ever will be.

I came away with something else you gave me
something that you said while we were talking,
talking of sunrise and birdsong.

Were you trying not to flirt with me that night,
describing something lovingly to me, or was it
something that you mentioned just in passing
something I had never seen but now
will always see in dawning daylight
as the birds awaken:

the early morning sun warming your naked back?

The Boss

Il capo di tutti i capi is a brute.
Though elegant, handsome and refined
his suit perfect
wearing scarlet at his throat
he has more than he can ever use
and guards it jealously.

No others are allowed near what he's claimed
as his, whether he has use for it or not.
Should any upstart encroach upon his turf
the interloper, in a flash, is gone.

But perhaps I've given him too grand a title
as he is merely *l'uccello di tutti gli uccelli*
a fine male specimen of Anna's Hummingbird
jealously guarding the feeder in my backyard
diving upon any other hummingbird that may approach
driving him away and over the fence
before he can take even one sip.

Then I learned he was even less than that
when the Traveler passed through—
a Rufous Hummingbird who makes his way
from Mexico, along the California coast
up to Alaska looking for a date.

When the Traveler appeared
our backyard brute bowed out
became as timid as you please
always deferring, waiting in a nearby tree
until the Traveler had drunk his fill.

The Traveler stayed in town a week
the former boss adjusted his routine
without complaint (or none that we could hear)

then the Traveler moved on
and His Nibs resumed his place
and his routine
perch, guard, chase, preen, drink
pretending to this day that nothing happened.

There's no point in my wondering what his mate thinks—
my Guide to Backyard Birds just says
"promiscuous."

To My Favorite Poet

The magician sliced his assistant in half
with a gleaming and well-polished smile,
then rolled her two sections to opposite ends
of the stage, and she sang all the while!

Reassembling her deftly, he took a deep bow—
we could see she was now quite intact.
The audience gasped in amazement and clapped
and begged to see more of their act.

It occurred to me
while I was watching their show
that if I had all the right gear
the mirrors, the boxes, the wires and the smoke
I might do the same in a year.

But you

you were the
lone man on the stage
who cut a carrot in half at ten paces
using nothing
but a playing card.

Sole Survivor

I shall command my words, my loyal retainers,
to march into the face of doubt and death
with or without fear I don't care

they will do as I say
(or they will say as I say)
not to be stopped by anything
not to be called back

or to be called back only by my realization
that they are a poor excuse for a lightning bolt,
a kiss, a first-opening of eyes, a cry, a lullaby,
a deluge, a rockslide, a shattering of sunlight
through a diamond.

Should I recklessly decide to let
my words continue on their way,
by the time they reach your gate
their clothes will be in tatters,
exhaustion will have nearly shut their eyes
and their feet will drag

and though they began their march
singing the song I long for you too to sing,
they will be mumbling tunelessly

and even if you lift the kerchief from your hair
and cup your ear and hold behind your lips
your sweet soft breath,
you may make out
at best, one word.

If you do, then *répondez s'il vous plaît*
and when the weary remnant of your expedition,
the last surviving word of your reply,
presents itself in rags at my gate
I will consider how to use it
in the poem I hope to write someday.

Creation

If one of my characters
declares that he has no free will
because I have already decided his fate
I will be annoyed
and destroy the manuscript

If another of my characters
claims to have logically proven
the fact of my existence
I will be mildly amused
and leave him to his own devices

But if one of my characters
disagrees with me
argues with me
looks me in the eye
and tells me where to go,
I'll just laugh

and keep writing.

Myringotomist of the Morning

Last night was good
words fail me

but this morning I have no trouble
finding a way to say that when I was three
and there were only two antibiotics available
for the treatment of otitis media
and I was allergic to both of them,
the only way the doctor knew
to relieve the pressure on my eardrum
was to lance it with a needle
and let the fluid out

my mother had to hold my head still
while the doctor did the thing
what I remember most vividly is
not the pain
but the loud inescapable scraping noise
the needle made
just before the doctor poked it
through my eardrum
and the feeling of bracing myself
against what was coming
like
(at the breakfast table this morning)
your voice.

Well-Mannered Thief

Jays' calls are screams and shouts and squawks, not songs.
I never would have thought they'd be polite.

The scrub-jay saw the bright red glow
of my tomatoes, picked out the one
hanging highest in the noonday sun
pecked at it until he broke the skin
and ate his fill, which wasn't very much.
He left no claw marks, did not bruise or foul
the unripe fruit remaining, did not peck
at anything he didn't plan to eat.

He came back every day and ate that same
tomato bit by bit until it was
an empty shell of red tomato skin.
So polite! He may come back for more
but I can count on his restraint—a thief
who steals from me one penny every day.
I took the fleeing flash of blue and gray
I barely saw as he made his escape
to be his thank-you note, his "By your leave!"

Might you have taken more from me each day?
The damage that is visible is slight.
Amid the leaves still green, the fruits still firm,
a limp red husk still hangs here in the sun.

They are that that talks of going...

To Robert Frost
on last reading his "The Sound of Trees"

A maple tree in deep shade
beneath an endless canopy of leaves
will not grow very tall—
it needs a patch of unobstructed sky
to reach for

meanwhile it waits
a century if need be
for one of its nearest neighbors to die
(a neighbor who might be a very close relative
since even the whirligig seed on the wind
doesn't fall far from the tree)
leaving a beckoning patch of blue
toward which the tree,
no longer young,
will grow with startling speed

meanwhile I
(without a century to spare
and hoping not to lose my nearest)
play with what lies at my feet,
and wonder at what there may be
just outside the circle
I can compass without pulling up my roots.

The Short Version

A Tale in Seven Senryu

closing my front door
I start my day as always
leaving all I love

fogged bathroom mirror
but I remember when we
steamed up our windshield

in the Labyrinth
trying in vain to recall
the first wrong turn

"I have no regrets"
"I would do it all again"
those are not the same

at the slightest push
the oars lost and the sails slack
our boats drift apart

old gate in the wind
bangs shut, but half of a latch
finds no mate, lets go

the gates rusted shut
the temple grounds abandoned
I still pray, outside

III

The End of the Tourist Season

summer bungalow
in winter, old empty wood—
soon, my hair's color

Milestones

They told me that my vision would get worse.
(Perhaps I should have told them, "Yes, I see.")

They told me that I would not hear as well.
(Perhaps I should have told them, "So I've heard.")

They told me time would rush by in a blur.
(Perhaps I should have asked them, "Come again?")

They told me I would miss my children too.
(Perhaps they knew I wouldn't think of that.)

They never told me (they must have assumed
I'd know) something I noticed only yesterday

that I would look at you and find you
breathtaking

still.

Pause

Our walks took us past
the caretaker's locked shack
where we always stood on tiptoe
and looked through the window
at the dusty tools and desk
and the calendar whose page
had not been turned in twenty years.

Tearing Out the Blue Girls

We dug the roses from their corner plot.
They'd done well there, but sadly we agreed
that we had erred severely in their placement
and thrown the yard's design into imbalance.
We tore them out.

But rootstock spread and sprouted, its rough pedigree
exposed for all to see. The elegance
of what was grafted to it, long since gone,
has been replaced by something old and tough
in colors we'd not planned, in shapes unbidden,
with leaves unlike the ones we'd hoped to see,
with thin and arching stems, not solid stalks,
and, unlike the roses we had killed,
with simple blossoms—just five petals each.
They come up where they will, and when, and how.
They'll still be there when all the rest is weeds,
wild grasses, asphalt rubble, stucco shards,
a barely recognizable foundation
and sun and dust
and wind and rain
and crickets.

Bête Noire

A cat is hunting a mouse
in the dark
just outside the squirrel's hollow tree

the squirrel
hopes that noise is not an owl
who sees better at night than the cat
who sees better at night than the mouse
who sees better at night than he does

the squirrel is too afraid of the owl
to write a poem about it

instead, he will write a poem
about the cat, or perhaps
about the mouse, who will
(tomorrow morning
when the sun is so bright
it would hurt his eyes if he went out)
stay in
and find himself unable
to write a poem
about the cat.

Teaching by Example

He took care of his beloved wife
for as long as he was able

longer than it takes to raise a child
longer than your favorite dog will live
longer than agave waits to flower

until the day he broke his wrist while bathing her
(the county workers came for her that day)
That done, there was little he could do
but sit by her and talk and hold her hand
as she went deeper, deeper into shadow

A night they said might be her last
found him in his customary place
sitting by her side
holding her hand and speaking softly to her
until the nurse came in
and tapped him gently on the shoulder

"You can let go now, sir. She's gone."

He refused the surgery
that might have given him more time—
time he no longer wanted

Within a year
a night they said might be his last
found him alone but for his only daughter
sitting by his side
holding his hand and speaking softly to him
until the nurse came in
and tapped her gently on the shoulder

"You can let go now."

Letter from California

This Fall I shall be homesick once again,
for forests saturated with the hues
of brilliant colored leaves, an awesome sight
that makes my grandest metaphor sound trite.

A watercolorist I once spoke with
said he found eastern autumns overwhelming;
the painting would be unbelievable.
(I imagine an exhilarated painter,
at first delighted with his forest's colors,
slowly—dazzled, puzzled and defeated—
packing up his easel for the season
not to return until a winter day
provides a more believable display.)

Passing Through

When I was five I thought I'd be a fireman.
As soon as I was old enough to say
"paleontologist,"
that was my goal.
Meteorologist,
astrophysicist,
veterinarian,
wildlife biologist,
all are on the list.

Look as I speed by, empty,
the landscape beyond showing through
like a passing boxcar
with the doors on both sides open.

Elegy for a Poet

Neither of us ever found the key
(hell, neither of us even found the door!)
but he helped me clean the windows now and then
which left my view much better than before.

Excuse Me, May I Have a Word?

I could use a metaphor right now.
Anybody got one to spare? Really,
I don't bum them very often but
I really need one
it's been too long and dammit
I'm nervous and jittery and
I'd lend you one if *you* asked
and really it would it really
would be just a loan
I absolutely promise that someday when
you really really really need one yourself
I will return it in better condition
than when you gave it to me.

And oh yeah—got a light?

Bird Netting

Her head was slightly cocked,
wind-ruffled feathers shedding drops of rain.
The way she'd entered to find shelter from the rain last year
was now impassible, yet visible.
This puzzled her beyond her small capacity for thought
and so she paced the ledge, a matter of a foot or so,
confused, but capable of wishing herself
inside last year's shelter from this year's weather.

She'd flown about the building where the nets had been installed
that kept her from establishing a newer perch,
so now she looked again at last year's roost
while images emerged (disjointed in her mind,
not strung together in life's narrative of self)
of a mate, and a dry nest cradling warm eggs.

Beneath Our Notice

I couldn't place the dusty bits of black
at first—too large for flyspecks,
too small for droppings of a mouse.
A closer look showed me a trail of ants
above the shelf, a bit below the ceiling.

A spider had established a position
next to the trail where she could grab an ant
at will. She had been dropping empty skins
of ants (if the integuments of ants
can be called skins) onto the shelf below.

I wondered how the spider chose her victims.
Was one ant more appealing than another?
Was she waiting for the weak to lag,
or waiting for the curious to stray?
And did she know or care that just below,
I watched, and swept the dust of death away?

Legacy

Here there is fog
just up the road
there was sun but
here there is fog

poppies hold buds closed
birds wait in silence
bees do not search
frogs hold their breaths

the thick gray air
grows moss on logs
and mold on paper,
makes water slower
and stones heavier

my mother told me
to come to this place
and wait—
my father too
they never told me
why.

Misunderstanding

She walked from room to room
at times unsteady on her aging feet
at times more sure.

Her wobbly gait did not upset her—
the cane was support enough
but something she could not quite put her finger on
still bothered her
something that she couldn't quite recall.

She examined floors and ceilings,
gazed out windows.
No...she gazed *at* windows, glass and frame,
inspected every wall

her glance caressing all the woodwork
with a practiced eye that one might call
both loving and professional

then finally she stopped before the mirror in the hall
where her husband found her weeping.

"You're still beautiful," he whispered
as he touched her shoulder gently.
She turned and brought him slowly into focus.

"That's not it at all.
When I was an architect
I designed this house.
I can't remember how."

Changing Seasons

Instead of rattling my window pane
(the way the one now letting herself out
by the back door, quietly, had done) she chose
instead to let a silver song announce
her coming, by a barely stirring brush
of scented hands against the old wind chimes
that hung on the front porch. I'd heard no step,
or voice, or knock, but opened the front door.

She asked—insisted—that I walk with her
and since I'd not the skill to lure her in,
gladly agreed. She showed me things I knew
but told me they were new, and I, convinced,
let her point out her birds, her trees, her flowers,
her frescoes of leaf-shadows on the fence,
her warmth and wind, her living, breathing soil,
her ferns, her field-mice, and her sunny sky.
She flirted constantly, made jokes about my seeds,
and urged me to plant something just for her.

Abruptly serious, she stopped and looked at me
with something between pain and resignation.
Behind her gaze it seemed as if she searched
for words a poor doomed fool could understand.
With voice like breeze and rainfall, not quite singing,
she said, "I am afraid that what we've tried
four times a year, in different ways, to tell you
you still do not believe, or understand.
Please try to comprehend this, one more time."

"Tell me, then," I said, "Why should I doubt you?"
She said, "One day I'll take this walk without you."

Patterns on a Schoolroom Floor

—for Professor Mary Rhodes Hoover, Howard University,
   a lifelong champion of universal literacy

You looked into the darkness of the shadow of the mountain
where some, tending their small fires, had not yet given up.

But when you saw the outline and the shape of that great shadow,
you turned around and *saw the mountain*;
and you said to all of us, "Let's *move* this thing!"

You didn't have the strength to move the mountain by yourself,
but like others who've moved mountains, you moved people,
and enough people come together can move mountains.

You showed us how, in life, great things are done
though life itself be short, and insubstantial
as the patterns of the interwoven sun and shadows
dancing in a circle on a schoolroom floor.

Parting Words

Fluent in four languages, my mother
lost the only one we understood,
her English pinched out like a candle wick
by another blood clot in her head.

Her French was still impeccable,
the nurse from Cameroon informed us,
but we understood no French.

I asked, in English, if she still knew German.
She replied in German,
one more language
we did not understand.

My mother's mother tongue, *mameh loshon,*
was Yiddish, 'til the age of six, and so
we guessed that it would be the last to go.

My brother found a neighbor who was fluent.
By then she wasn't speaking
and her eyes were closed.

I wasn't with her at the end. I'd like to think
that as she went where nobody could follow,
she recognized as hers something familiar,
whether sense, or syllable, or sound,
in whatever it was the stranger said to her.

Harbor Dreams

The pier feels the bump and scrape and jostle
almost awakened from its sleep, it dreams
again of stories told by roving ships

of fish as big as boats, of whales as big
as ships, of waves as big as flowing mountain
ranges, of forests without roots

the stories were exciting, captivating
but ultimately unbelievable
(you know what tall tales roving ships can tell)

the pier, embedded firmly in the mud
no longer bothers to awaken when
a ship ties up
but oh, the dreams,
the harbor dreams!

Acknowledgments

The author wishes to thank the editors of the publications in which these poems first appeared or are forthcoming, often in earlier forms:

"The Nietzsche Contrapositive" won the *Grey Sparrow Journal*'s 2014 Flash and Poetry Competition and appeared in the five year anniversary issue of the annual, *Snow Jewel*. Special thanks to the editor, Diane Smith, and to the judges, Mandi Casolo, Doug Holder, and Townsend Walker.

"A Little Night Music," "The End of the Tourist Season," "First Date with Athena," "at the slightest push" and "old gate in the wind," published as *The Owl at Sunset*, a Leaflet edition, Leaf Press, Vancouver, Canada.

The Bicycle Review: "Bête Noir"
Benicia Herald: "Fallow," "Sculpture"
Convergence: "Revisiting," "Aerial Survey" (previously titled "Biological Control"), "The Full Set"
Forge: "Introduction to Crop Management"
Glassworks: "Bird Netting," "Wisteria from Seed"
Heyday Magazine: "Myringotomist of the Morning," "Tough Times"
Naugatuck River Review: "Display Case"
Pirene's Fountain: "Parting Words"
Poetalk: "Differential Diagnosis"
Printer's Devil Review: "Deference"
Prospectus: "What This Dog Thinks," "Why Don't You Finish Anything You Start?"

"Tearing Out the Blue Girls" (previously titled "The Garden Evolves"), "Patterns on a Schoolroom Floor" and "Changing Seasons" originally appeared in the anthology *Yesterdays,* Rock and Feather Publications, 2007.

"Milestones," "Teaching by Example," "Creation" and "To My Favorite Poet" originally appeared in the anthology *Current Shores*, edited by Robert Shelby, Samizdat Press & Southampton House, 2009.

Special thanks to:

My mentors, whose assistance in the preparation of this book and in my development as a writer have been indispensable—fine poets, good friends and an inspiration to me, every one: Joel Fallon, the first poet laureate of Benicia, California, where I live and where I first read in public (with trembling hands); Robert Shelby, the second poet laureate of Benicia, who never plays with the net down; Connie Post, host of the superb Valona Deli Poetry Series, a venue that has enabled me to make my work known and to hear the best poets passing through or living in the San Francisco Bay Area; and Peter Bray, the poet and friend who gave me the wisteria seeds.

Michael Manning, who knows the place where music, science and poetry meet.

Robert Aquinas McNally, who finds and reveals the poetry in Linnaeus.

All the poets in the Benicia First Tuesday Poetry Group, especially Lois Requist, the fourth poet laureate of Benicia, who convinced me not to wait.

My readers and family, whose enthusiastic response to my work has been a constant inspiration.

And very special thanks to Karen Kelsay of Kelsay Books for choosing this book (my first), and for her guidance through these unfamiliar woods.

I am particularly grateful to my parents, who surrounded me with words, music and art—particularly to my mother, who read *everything* to me, from *The Color Kittens* to *The Catcher in the Rye*. I wish they had lived to see the creation of this, my first book.

And countless thanks to my wife, Marsha, without whom this book would not exist.

About the Author

Jeremy Cantor began writing poetry shortly before retiring from a career in laboratory chemistry. He has cleared tables and washed dishes, made and tested detergents, pharmaceuticals and engine oil additives, driven a forklift, spent time in a full-body acid-proof hazmat suit, tried to keep his fingers working in a walk-in freezer at -40°F and worked behind radiation shielding. He prefers writing.

His poem, "The Nietzsche Contrapositive," won the *Grey Sparrow Journal*'s 2014 Flash & Poetry Competition. A Leaflet edition of his haiku and senryu, *The Owl at Sunset*, is forthcoming from Leaf Press, Vancouver, Canada. Jeremy's work has appeared in *The Naugatuck River Review*, *Printer's Devil Review*, *Pirene's Fountain*, *Glassworks*, *The Bicycle Review, Prospectus* and other publications.

Jeremy was born and raised in Connecticut, attended the University of Michigan in Ann Arbor, and now lives with his wife in a small town on a tidal strait connecting the Sacramento River with San Francisco Bay. Summer evenings he goes fishing downtown from the pier at the foot of First Street, while the sun sets behind the bridge and the sea lions dive for salmon.